Biomes
of the World

TAIGA

ELIZABETH KAPLAN

BENCHMARK BOOKS

MARSHALL CAVENDISH
NEW YORK

Benchmark Books
Marshall Cavendish Corporation
99 White Plains Road
Tarrytown, New York 10591-9001

©Marshall Cavendish Corporation, 1996

Series created by Blackbirch Graphics, Inc.

For Steve—Maybe we can visit the taiga together someday.—Beth

Printed in Hong Kong.

Library of Congress Cataloging-in-Publication Data

Kaplan, Elizabeth.
    Taiga / Elizabeth Kaplan.
        p.   cm. — (Biomes of the world)
    Includes bibliographical references (p.   ) and index.
    Summary: Describes climate, soil, seasons, and landscape of the
world's largest continuous biome which spans the Northern Hemisphere
across Alaska, Canada, Scandinavia, and Russia.
    ISBN 0-7614-0135-0
    1. Taiga ecology—Juvenile literature. 2. Taigas—Juvenile literature.
[1. Taigas. 2. Forest ecology. 3. Ecology.] I. Title. II. Series.
QH541.5.T3K36   1996
574.5'2642—dc20   95-38923
                                               CIP
                                               AC

Contents

Introduction

People traveling in an airplane often marvel at the patchwork patterns they see as they look down on the land. Fields, forests, grasslands, and deserts, each with its own identifiable color and texture, form a crazy quilt of varying designs. Ecologists—scientists who study the relationship between living things and their environment—have also observed the repeating patterns of life that appear across the surface of the earth. They have named these geographical areas biomes. A biome is defined by certain environmental conditions and by the plants and animals that have adapted to these conditions.

The map identifies the earth's biomes and shows their placement across the continents. Most of the biomes are on land. They include the tropical rainforest, temperate forest, grassland, tundra, taiga, chaparral, and desert. Each has a unique climate, including yearly patterns of temperature, rainfall, and sunlight, as well as certain kinds of soil. In addition to the land biomes, the oceans of the world make up a single biome, which is defined by its salt-water environment.

Looking at biomes helps us understand the interconnections between our planet and the living things that inhabit it. For example, the tilt of the earth on its axis and wind patterns both help to determine the climate of any particular biome.

The climate, in turn, has a great impact on the types of plants that can flourish, or even survive, in an area. That plant life influences the composition and stability of the soil. And the soil, in turn, influences which plants will thrive. These inter-connections continue in every aspect of nature. While some animals eat plants, others use plants for shelter or conceal-ment. And the types of plants that grow in a biome directly influence the species of animals that live there. Some of the animals help pollinate plants. Many of them enrich the soil with their waste.

Within each biome, the interplay of climatic conditions, plants, and animals defines a broad pattern of life. All of these interactions make the plants and animals of a biome interde-pendent and create a delicate natural balance. Recognizing these different relationships and how they shape the natural world enables us to appreciate the complexity of life on Earth and the beauty of the biomes of which we are a part.

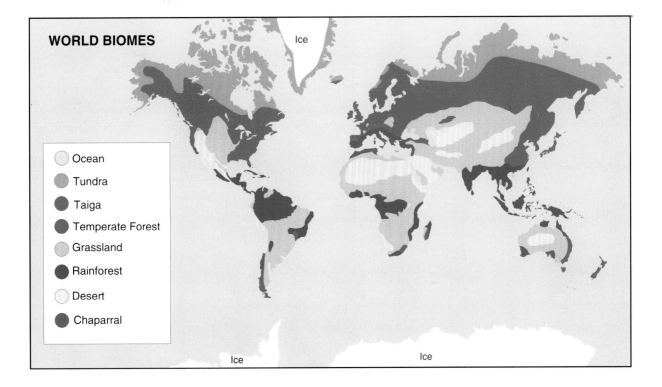

WORLD BIOMES

Ice

Ocean
Tundra
Taiga
Temperate Forest
Grassland
Rainforest
Desert
Chaparral

Ice

Ice

1

The Northern Forest

Imagine crossing over the taiga, or the boreal forest, in a small plane. The spires of spruce trees stand straight and tall. Lakes lie scattered among the thick trees, sparkling like jewels. An occasional stand of quaking aspen or white birch trees shimmers in the sunshine, marking a region that decades ago was burned to the ground by a forest fire. Only rarely does the narrow ribbon of a road make an appearance. Instead, the vast expanse of the taiga's coniferous forest stretches across the horizon in an endless carpet of evergreen.

Opposite: This watery landscape in Canada's Northwest Territory shows swampy muskeg vegetation and small trees typical of the taiga landscape.

7

Taiga is the Russian word for "marshy pine forest." In many ways, the taiga is the world's most pristine forest. Spanning the Northern Hemisphere in a wide swath across Alaska, Canada, Scandinavia, and Russia, the taiga also forms the world's largest continuous biome. Because of its size and its remote location, far north of most of the world's big cities, the taiga has so far escaped the extensive damage that the temperate and tropical forests have suffered. However, the taiga's cold climate and northern location also make it one of the world's most fragile biomes. Only a few species of trees can thrive in the taiga, and not many animals can live there year-round. If an area is damaged by fire, disease, or logging, centuries will pass before the tall, majestic spruce and fir trees tower again in the taiga.

Climate and Light Conditions in the Taiga

The climate of the taiga is one of the most extreme in the world. In the winter, temperatures can drop below -76°F (-60°C). In the summer, they can rise above 104°F (40°C). Plants and animals that inhabit the taiga throughout the year have to adapt to each extreme, a variation that may be more than 180°F (82°C).

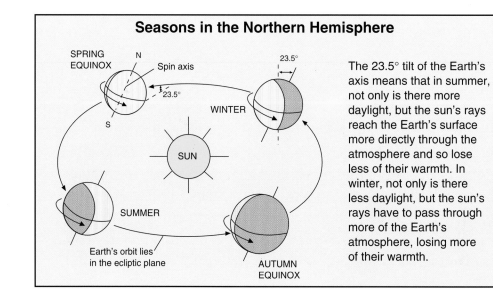

Seasons in the Northern Hemisphere

SPRING EQUINOX

N

Spin axis

23.5°

23.5°

S

WINTER

SUN

SUMMER

Earth's orbit lies in the ecliptic plane

AUTUMN EQUINOX

The 23.5° tilt of the Earth's axis means that in summer, not only is there more daylight, but the sun's rays reach the Earth's surface more directly through the atmosphere and so lose less of their warmth. In winter, not only is there less daylight, but the sun's rays have to pass through more of the Earth's atmosphere, losing more of their warmth.

A meadow vole peeks out of the thick snow that insulates it from the extreme cold.

Light levels also fluctuate widely. This is because the taiga is located in the upper latitudes of the Earth. During summer in the taiga, the Northern Hemisphere is tilted toward the sun. Because of its location—the northern part of the Northern Hemisphere—the taiga is bathed in light, sometimes for twenty hours a day. The sun sits on the horizon for long

THE MONTANE BOREAL FOREST

If you live in a mountainous region, you can visit a forest much like the taiga without having to travel to the northern reaches of the Northern Hemisphere. All you have to do is make your way up the side of a mountain. If you live in a very moist or tropical region, you will probably start out in a rainforest. As you hike, you will soon find yourself in a deciduous forest. If you continue on your way, you will come to an evergreen forest. At first, pines may predominate in this forest. As you go up the mountain, though, you will probably begin to see more spruce and fir trees. Near the upper edge of this taigalike forest, the trees will get smaller and will stand farther apart. By this time, you will have hiked upward about 3,000 feet (914 meters) in elevation. You will look out on the alpine tundra. With your hike up the mountain, you will have covered a journey through many of the Earth's major biomes.

The montane boreal forest, as this coniferous forest is called, differs from the taiga in several ways. Water drains rapidly off the mountain rather than building up in bogs or the muskeg, as it does in the taiga. Because of this, the soil of the montane boreal forest tends to be fairly dry. The length of a day is more constant in the mountains of more southerly latitudes. Thus, the montane boreal forest gets more sunlight and more high-intensity light than the taiga does. Winds tend to be stronger on the mountainside than they are on the taiga, but both regions have harsh climates.

Hikers enjoy a walk in the montane boreal forest in British Columbia, Canada.

periods of time around sunrise and sunset. The low light filters through the needles of the spruce and fir trees, giving the taiga a deep, warm glow. During winter in the taiga, the Northern Hemisphere is tilted away from the sun. Light reaches the biome for only a few hours in the middle of the day. This lack of sunlight makes the forest a dark, frigid, gloomy place.

Because temperatures are low for many months of the year, the taiga does not receive large amounts of annual precipitation. (Cold air does not hold moisture as well as warm air does, so clouds do not form as easily and rain and snow do not fall as readily in cold regions.) The snow that does fall, though, may stay on the ground for six months or longer. The trees of the taiga form a barrier against the wind, so the snow does not blow away, as it does on the tundra.

The snow forms a layer several feet thick in places, which shelters and insulates many taiga animals and plants. Snow crystals contain spaces in which air gets trapped. This air remains at a temperature of about 32°F (0°C), at or just below freezing. This air is often much warmer than the outside air. The plants and animals that live under the snow are protected from the extreme cold of the taiga winter.

Soggy, Acidic Soils

The climate has a direct effect on the soil of the taiga. Because of the extreme cold, some areas of the taiga have an underlying layer of permanently frozen ground, which is known as permafrost. Water from rain and melting snow cannot seep through the permafrost. It remains in the upper layers of the soil, making the soil soft and soggy. Other areas of the taiga have an underlying layer of very hard rock close to the surface of the land. In North America, this rock layer is called the Canadian Shield. As with the permafrost, this dense rock prevents water from soaking deep into the ground. In the spring and summer, therefore, the thin layer of soil above this rocky shield is usually soaked with water.

The rock of the Canadian Shield, shown here in Ontario, Canada, prevents water from soaking into the ground when the ice melts in the summer.

The climate of the taiga affects not only the levels of the moisture in its soil but also the composition of its soil. Soil is a mixture of minerals and organic material from plant and animal tissues that have decomposed. Since the taiga is covered with coniferous trees, needles from these trees are the predominant leaf litter. These leaves have a thick, waxy coat and fragrant resins that take a long time to decompose in the cold climate of the taiga. Thus, soil forms very slowly in this biome.

The soil that does form is highly acidic. This is because conifer needles have a high acid content. Acids are released into the soil when the needles begin to rot on the ground. In addition, as water in the soggy surface layer of the ground seeps deeper into the soil, it leaches the scant amount of nutrients from this upper layer. The soil becomes a fine ashen powder in which few plants can grow.

The Taiga Landscape

The soggy, acidic soil of the taiga makes for a unique landscape, one dominated by only a few types of trees. White spruce and black spruce are the two main species of trees found throughout the taiga. In western North America, jack pines mix in with the spruces. In eastern North America, balsam fir is the third most common tree of the taiga. In eastern Asia, the larch, a conifer that drops its leaves in the winter, ranges widely with the spruces. In most parts of the taiga, the forest floor is covered with a soft carpet of moss. A few bushes and other small plants grow under the dense canopy of the conifer branches.

But it is the ground itself that makes the taiga landscape especially surprising. In many parts of the taiga, the ground is more liquid than solid. This is because much of the taiga is made up of bogs in various stages of being filled in. In some places, there is the open water of a small, pristine lake. In other places, water plants mat shallow ponds, creating an ideal environment for mosquitoes and dragonflies. In still other

Mosses and ferns carpet this bog of balsam fir and black spruce.

places, grasses, mosses, and even spruce trees grow on the semi-firm soil, which is tricky for hikers to negotiate. A step onto what looks like a firm, moss-covered path may result in one's sinking into brown water that rises over the ankles. This oozing wet ground is known as the muskeg, and it is a unique feature of the taiga landscape.

From the Temperate Forest to the Tundra

The taiga spans tremendous distances, not only from east to west—across the continents of North America, Europe, and Asia—but also from north to south—from the tundra to

THE DRUNKEN FOREST

In some parts of the muskeg, you can step onto a mat of moss and watch the spruce trees teeter around you. This is not an illusion. The trees that grow on the muskeg have very shallow roots that grow no deeper than the thickness of the moss layer, perhaps only a few inches. When you step on the moss, you essentially cause an earthquake in the muskeg, and the trees rock back and forth in response. This unstable marshy woods is nicknamed the drunken forest.

During winter, the muskeg forest may assume what looks like a permanently drunken state. When water freezes, the frost can cause the ground to push up in mounds. The trees growing in the frozen ground are pushed out at an angle. They may remain tilted until the ground thaws in the spring.

Sometimes, however, the ground does not return to its previous position. A hummock (a rounded knoll) forms, and a tree grows sideways. If the tree remains in this position for several growing seasons, the trunk will curve so that the tree is once more growing upright. Should the ground heave with frost again and cause the hummock to collapse, the trunk will curve to compensate for the shift in the ground level. Many trees of the muskeg have S-shaped trunks as a result, which adds to the drunken look of the forest.

Supports are necessary to hold up these telephone poles in the muskeg of Manitoba, Canada. If the poles are put in straight, they often sink too far down to be of use.

the temperate forest. In many places, the taiga covers close to 2,000 miles (3,200 kilometers) north to south. At its southern edge, the taiga blends with the temperate forest. Hardwood, deciduous trees—those that lose their leaves—such as maple, beech, ash, and dogwood, mix with the coniferous trees. Farther north, pines mix with the spruces that dominate the taiga biome.

Gradually, the deciduous trees thin out and, with the exception of stands of aspen and birch, eventually disappear. The aspen and birch spring up in areas of the taiga that have been cleared by felled trees, diseases, or forest fires. In other regions, the spruce, pine, and other conifers of the taiga stretch northward in what seems like an endless forest. In some places, the wind swirls around rocky outcrops or over sheer cliffs of granite, and the trees, unable to withstand the continual blasts, may thin out. Lakes, marshes, and bogs dot the forest in other areas. Throughout most of the taiga, however, the branches of the conifers intertwine, throwing the ground into deep shade.

Continuing northward, the forest becomes more and more patchy. Tall trees grow in clumps in sheltered spots and along the banks of some lakes and rivers. Less protected areas are often covered with miniature spruce, willow, and birch trees growing along the ground in shrubby mats. Occasionally, a single spruce tree grows above a mat, but most of the trees are mowed down by strong winds. This region of the taiga is called the krummholz, a German term meaning "crooked wood."

Although the trees of the krummholz are small, some may be more than one hundred years old. The krummholz marks the boundary between the taiga and the tundra, the treeless biome of arctic regions. The taiga, however, may extend far into the tundra along riverbanks where the underlying layer of permafrost is not continuous. Here, trees can extend their roots deeper into the ground and water is more readily available.

Opposite: Here, the end of the northern boreal forest blends with the beginning of the tundra in Denali National Park, Alaska.

2

Spring and Summer in the Taiga

The seasons contrast sharply with one another in the taiga. Winter, with its heavy blanket of snow, its silent frozen lakes, and its subzero temperatures, usually lasts for six to seven months. Summer is a short, hot blaze—three to four months of mosquitoes, blackflies, blueberries, and songbirds twittering in the conifers. Fall is a brief transition from flowing water to frozen streams, and from soft, oozing mud and spongy moss to ice-hardened ground. Spring brings the creaks and groans of melting ice and the honks of geese and other waterfowl returning to the lakes and marshes of the northern woods.

Opposite: Spring is the birthing time for many animals in the taiga. Here, a cow moose wades in the water with her young calf.

19

Life Bursts Forth in the Taiga

In early March, long before the snow has melted and water flows freely in the river, life bursts forth in the taiga with the arrival of longer, warmer spring days. Red squirrels make forays from their nests high in the trees. They scamper across the snow, looking for fallen pinecones, which they pick apart for the seeds. Their tracks zigzag from tree to tree, and their activity increases as the weather warms up. Red squirrels may give birth to litters of three to five young between late March and May. The young remain safe in the nest until they are strong enough to climb down from the trees.

Another taiga animal that gives birth in early spring is the wolverine. Although its name gives the impression that the wolverine is related to the wolf, this rare resident of the far north is really the largest member of the weasel family. The wolverine, however, looks nothing like its relatives. It is not sleek but chunky. Its face is wide and bearish, rather than long and pointed. Although it is less than 2 feet (1 meter) tall, the wolverine is strong enough to kill a 9-foot-tall (3-meter-tall) moose. It is so fierce that it can drive off bears trying to steal its kill. In mid- to late March, wolverines find a protected spot, such as a rock crevice, in which to give birth. The young stay with their mothers throughout the spring and for the next two years. During this time, they learn to become expert hunters of the taiga night.

Other members of the weasel family that roam the

The fierce wolverine gives birth in early spring.

taiga—martens, ermines, minks, and river otters—also give birth in the early spring. Young gray wolves are born a little later, in April or May. Red foxes give birth to their young then as well. By this time, the snow has melted away in the sunny, open areas of the taiga. The ground has started to thaw. The ice is thinning or breaking up on the lakes and rivers. The branches of conifer trees sway freely in the warm breeze, their heavy mantles of snow having fallen to the ground with a thud.

The Silent Spring

One of the most profound changes of spring takes place in silence. As snow drops from the branches of the conifers and moisture seeps into the dried-up beds of moss carpeting the ground, these plants come to life. Because they keep their leaves year-round, evergreen trees are always ready to make food by the process of photosynthesis. This process takes place inside any plant cells that contain a green pigment called chlorophyll. In evergreens and in most other trees, chlorophyll is found in the leaves, where it traps sunlight for a tree. The tree uses the energy from the sunlight to combine carbon dioxide and water, producing a simple sugar called glucose. Glucose provides the tree's source of energy for all of its life processes.

A red squirrel brings food to her young as they wait in the safety of their warm nest.

21

THE BUSY BEAVER

In a clearing, a small pond glows orange as the setting sun reflects off the water. Near the middle of the pond, is a large mound of sticks with a hidden underwater entrance. This is a lodge, home to one of the taiga's busiest residents—the beaver. If you listen closely, you may hear a trickle of water running through the dam at the edge of the pond. Under cover of darkness, the beavers that live in the lodge will swim out to repair the hole in the dam. Until then, though, the pond is peacefully silent.

Beavers create entire environments that help them survive well in the watery north woods. They back up streams by building dams of sticks and mud. In time, beaver dams become so stable that grass grows on them. The largest beaver dams stand 7 feet (2 meters) above the original water level and are so strong that people can walk or even ride horses across them. Generally, the only way to destroy these examples of the beaver's engineering ability is with a bulldozer or dynamite.

Beavers construct a snug home protected from predators in the beaver pond. The beaver lodge is a stick-and-mud mound with a hollow space that extends above the water. The floor of the lodge is just above the level of the water, with a hole that serves as an underwater entrance. Beavers dig tunnels from the banks of the pond, under the water, to their lodge. These secret entrances help keep them safe from predators. They also keep a pile of twigs near the underwater entrance to the lodge, both as a store of food when predators lurk and as a winter supply of food.

Snow and ice can damage beaver lodges and dams. The expanding ice can cause cracks in these structures. Beavers spend a lot of time in the spring making repairs. They reinforce their dams and lodges with sticks. They apply mud to repair leaks. Beavers also fell trees to replenish their stores of food and building materials. Exerting a broad influence on the taiga landscape, beavers can alter the flow of streams, and change the entire composition of the surrounding forest with their activities.

Beavers build extremely strong dams and lodges—often strong enough for a person to walk on.

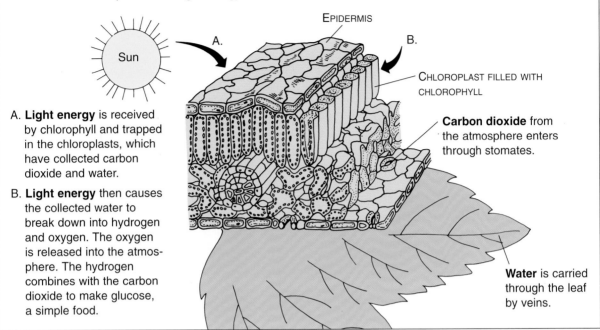

PHOTOSYNTHESIS

A plant needs light energy, water, and carbon dioxide to make its own food.

EPIDERMIS

A.

B.

CHLOROPLAST FILLED WITH CHLOROPHYLL

Sun

A. Light energy is received by chlorophyll and trapped in the chloroplasts, which have collected carbon dioxide and water.

B. Light energy then causes the collected water to break down into hydrogen and oxygen. The oxygen is released into the atmosphere. The hydrogen combines with the carbon dioxide to make glucose, a simple food.

Carbon dioxide from the atmosphere enters through stomates.

Water is carried through the leaf by veins.

Evergreen trees, including the spruce, fir, and pine trees of the taiga, can carry out photosynthesis whenever the temperature of their leaves climbs a few degrees above freezing. The needles of these trees are dark in color and so heat up when sunlight hits them. Even in the early spring, when temperatures in the taiga are still below zero, the evergreens may be able to photosynthesize. The needles trap the low light that is reflected beneath the branches of the trees. When the snow falls off the branches later in the spring, the evergreens become even more active and efficient food factories for the forest.

The mosses that carpet the forest floor become active a little later in the spring. They dry out in the fall so that their delicate tissues are not destroyed. (Freezing water would burst the mosses' cells.) As the ice thaws and the snow melts in mid-spring, the mosses are soaked with water, which they absorb. Because mosses keep their green pigments throughout the winter, they can begin to photosynthesize once they are rehydrated. Like the evergreens of the taiga, the mosses get a head start on summer.

By mid-May, most goshawks have returned to the taiga.

Animals Coming and Going

By the middle of May, the taiga swarms with life. Ducks, geese, and other waterfowl have returned to the taiga from their warmer winter homes to the south. They nest in the tall grasses around bogs and marshes and swim on the ice-free waters of the open lakes. Goshawks and red-tailed hawks have also made their way back to the northern woods. They perch in the trees and keep a sharp eye out for the mice, lemmings, voles, and small birds that make up their diet. Songbirds, such as yellow-bellied sapsuckers, red-breasted nut-hatches, golden and ruby-crowned kinglets, robins, hermit thrushes, cedar waxwings, and a variety of vireos and warblers flit through the trees and hop about on the ground. They build their nests and lay their eggs. The seeds of conifer trees, the fruits and berries that develop on the shrubs and bushes, and the hordes of hatching insects provide plentiful food for the taiga's summer migrants.

Rich as the taiga is during summer, some of its residents still migrate northward to the tundra before the summer season begins. In the spring, large herds of caribou head for secluded nesting grounds on the still-frozen tundra. These barren-ground caribou will spend the summer browsing on the crusty patches of lichen and tough grasses that carpet the rocky ground.

Many wolves that live in the taiga during the winter follow the caribou northward for the summer. Some, however, stay in the forest. These predators go after moose, deer, wood bison, and woodland caribou—endangered cousins of the barren-ground caribou. Woodland caribou are smaller than the barren-ground caribou, and they gather in small groups. In the United States, where they were once fairly common in the western Rockies, their numbers have decreased drastically due to overhunting, the clearing of the forests, and infection with a fatal parasite. At present, the taiga is the woodland caribou's only refuge.

The Time of Plenty

Summer is a brief time of plenty in the taiga. Plants take advantage of the long hours of daylight and grow profusely in the taiga's bogs and marshes. Water lilies cover the ponds. Moose wade in and dip their muzzles into the water to bring up

An Alaskan cow moose takes advantage of the plentiful summer vegetation.

mouthfuls of vegetation. They submerge themselves to escape from the mosquitoes and flies that swarm in the taiga through-out the summer.

Summer is the most productive season for insects. Their populations burgeon into the trillions. Some insects lay their eggs in the bark and needles of the conifers. When the larvae hatch, they have a ready supply of food—they eat the wood or the leaves around them. Woodpeckers, tits, and many of the migrant birds that inhabit the trees feast on these insects and their larvae. Other insects lay their eggs on or near the water. Their larvae are usually aquatic and feed on plants and other insects in small ponds. As the larvae grow, they change from swimming wormlike creatures to stinging winged adults. These insects provide food for many types of fish, which leap out of the water to snap them up. Birds also swoop and dive to catch the insects.

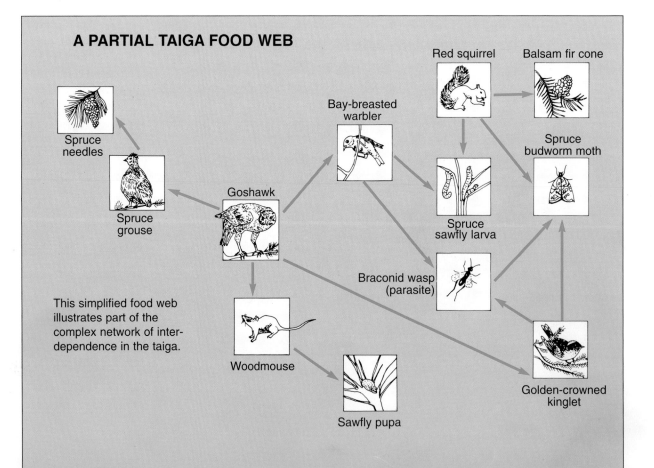

A PARTIAL TAIGA FOOD WEB

Spruce needles

Spruce grouse

Goshawk

Bay-breasted warbler

Red squirrel

Balsam fir cone

Spruce budworm moth

Spruce sawfly larva

Braconid wasp (parasite)

Woodmouse

Sawfly pupa

Golden-crowned kinglet

This simplified food web illustrates part of the complex network of inter-dependence in the taiga.

THE VOYAGEUR LIFESTYLE

In the eighteenth and nineteenth centuries, long-distance travel in the taiga was done almost exclusively by the voyageurs. These French-Canadian canoeists were employed by trading companies, such as the Hudson's Bay Company, to transport furs thousands of miles from remote outposts in the taiga to a trading post at Grand Portage, on the northern shores of Lake Superior. There, they picked up other trade goods, such as pots, kettles, blankets, guns, and ammunition, and paddled back to the farthest reaches of the north woods. The total length of the trip was more than 4,000 miles (6,400 kilometers) long.

Voyageurs made this journey over five months, from the beginning of May to the beginning of October. This was the only time that the ice did not block the waterways. Traveling sixteen to eighteen hours a day, the voyageurs covered an average daily distance of almost 30 miles (48 kilometers). They paddled up fast-flowing streams and down treacherous rapids. They spent days crossing storm-whipped lakes. They heaved their heavy loads along mud-soft portages, unable to swat at the swarms of mosquitoes that buzzed around their faces. But the voyageurs loved the independence their lifestyle gave them and the challenges of traveling through the taiga. The woods rang with their songs as they patched their birch-bark canoes late into the night.

The food web on the previous page shows the feeding relationships among many of the different organisms that live in the taiga during summer. Note that the arrows point from the organism that does the eating to the one that is eaten. This shows how energy is transferred throughout the taiga. For example, an arrow points from the spruce grouse to the spruce needles. This indicates that the spruce grouse gets its energy from eating the needles of the spruce tree. What do the warbler and the kinglet eat?

Summer's warmth creates an abundance of insects that support many of the taiga's residents. But as fall approaches and temperatures drop, the insects go into a state of dormancy, during which they burrow in the wood of trees or crawl deep underground. A sudden cold snap at the end of August can kill off the hardiest of insects. Summer wanes quickly in the taiga, and residents and migrants alike make preparations for the upcoming seasons of cold and snow.

3

Fall and Winter in the Taiga

It is late September. Large herds of barren-ground caribou file southward from the tundra. Packs of wolves follow them, sometimes at a close range, sometimes at a distance. Winter has begun in the northernmost biome. Frost has hardened the ground. Snow swirls in the air. Berries hang frozen on the bushes. In the taiga, however, the air is a little warmer, and the wind does not howl as fiercely as it does on the tundra. The taiga provides shelter for some summer residents of the tundra as well as for the many animals that will remain in the taiga throughout the year.

Opposite:
The foliage of aspen trees amid coniferous trees in the montane boreal forest signifies the onset of fall, as in the taiga.

29

The Sounds of Autumn

The birch and aspen trees of the forest turn yellow in the fall. The drooping leaves of the willow trees turn brown. But one of the clearest signs that autumn has come to the taiga is not the color change of the scattered groves of deciduous trees but a sound—the deep bellowing of bull moose during the mating season. Bulls lock antlers in fierce fights to determine which of them will mate with the females. These battles will continue throughout the month of September.

Female moose, which are pregnant during the fall and winter, give birth in the spring. This gives the young a longer span of time in which to grow strong and put on weight, which will help them survive the following winter. Like moose, caribou also mate in the fall, and their calves are born in the spring.

Two young bull moose lock antlers in battle.

Feasting Before the Famine

Autumn's chill drives the animals of the taiga to prepare for winter. Many of the waterfowl and the songbirds scramble to feast on late August's abundance of insects, berries, and seeds. Within the month, they will head for warmer nesting grounds far to the south. Some birds cover thousands of miles in their fall migration. They will use up their fat reserves on this difficult journey.

Many of the mammals of the taiga also gorge themselves in the late summer. Like the migrating birds, they need extra fat for insulation as well as for energy reserves to draw on during the long, cold, lean winter season. Moose munch on water plants and plant shoots in the spring and summer, but they switch to twigs, berries, and conifer branches after the fall

A black bear expertly catches a salmon. Many animals of the taiga stock up on food before the arrival of winter.

freeze. A moose can eat 60 pounds (27 kilograms) of vegetation in a single day.

Similarly, black bears feed ferociously on the taiga's late-summer and early-autumn bounty. They snatch salmon that are swimming upriver to spawn. They graze through acres of berry patches. They catch rodents scurrying to gather their own stores of food. In a short amount of time, bears put on many pounds of fat for the winter. In their dens, the bears will live off of their fat during their long winter's resting period. Because their body temperatures remain close to normal, bears are not true hibernators. Instead, they go into a deep sleep that lasts most of the winter.

Stocking Up for Winter

Squirrels and chipmunks also use the fall to prepare for the winter. However, these animals cannot store food as fat reserves in their bodies. Instead, they collect seeds, nuts, and cones and bury them in underground caches. Squirrels, which remain active throughout the winter, dig up these supplies when they can no longer find or reach cones hanging on the trees.

Chipmunks, on the other hand, go into a state of hibernation during which their body temperatures drop almost to the freezing point. Before entering this dormancy, they bring the food they have gathered into their burrows. When they periodically rouse from hibernation, they have a ready supply of food to help them make it through the long winter.

Changing Color

The snowshoe hare responds to winter by growing a thick coat of white fur. The fur grows in slowly and provides camouflage in the fall. The hare's mottled coat of brown and white enables it to blend in with the patchy snow cover of the taiga in the early fall. As autumn wears on, more and more snow blankets the ground and the hare's white fur covers more and more of its coat. By the time winter arrives, the hare is

Top: During most of the year, the weasel's coat is brown and white, which provides camouflage against rocks and vegetation. Bottom: In the winter, the weasel, now called an ermine, has a coat of pure white, which makes it almost invisible against the snow.

completely white, well camouflaged against the snow. Weasels, which are called ermine in the winter, and ptarmigan, which are the chickenlike birds of the taiga, undergo similar changes in color throughout autumn.

CRAFTS OF THE OJIBWA

Imagine sitting in a wigwam made of birch bark, warming your hands in front of a fire of poplar wood, decorating moose-hide moccasins with dyed porcupine quills, and listening to legends of the clever animals of the north woods. This winter scene could have occurred thousands of years ago in the forest just north of Lake Superior. But it also takes place today, at the re-created Ojibwa Indian settlement at Old Fort Williams in Ontario, Canada. Here, in a reconstruction from the early 1800s, artisans employ traditional materials and techniques to craft all sorts of Ojibwa objects. In the summer, these artisans demonstrate basket weaving, burl carving, and bowl making to the many visitors who come to the fort. In the winter, some of the artisans teach their crafts to local residents and to people who have traveled long distances to learn about the Ojibwa.

The Ojibwa tribe was one of a number of Native American groups that made their home in the taiga. Members of these groups knew how to use the forest's resources for their survival while maintaining a deep reverence for the land. For instance, they gathered spruce roots to make a strong thread that was resistant to rot. By collecting only the thinnest roots and replacing the disturbed moss, they took care not to harm the trees. They offered prayers of thanksgiving to the individual trees that they harvested. Native Americans knew that their own survival depended on the protection of all the plants and animals that made up the complex network of the entire forest.

The Season of Snow

By the end of November, most parts of the taiga are covered by a foot or more of snow. The migrants have already flown south. The bugle calls of the moose's mating season have long since ceased. The chipmunks lie dormant in their burrows. The bears are entering their dens for their winter's rest. Even the squirrels spend most of the day sheltered in their nests, rarely climbing down from the trees. The forest is eerily silent, and the snow keeps on falling.

The conifers that dominate the taiga have unique adaptations that help them survive this season of snow and cold. Surprisingly, it is not the frigid temperatures that threaten these trees the most. It is the lack of water available to them.

Although trees constantly lose water through its evaporation from their leaves, they replenish their supply by absorbing water from the ground through their roots. In the winter, however, trees cannot do this, because the water is frozen in the ground. The shape of conifer leaves helps reduce the problem of evaporation. The needles present a smaller surface area to the sun and wind, so they lose little water to evaporation. In addition, conifer needles have a waxy coating that also helps to hold in water. With these adaptations, conifers are able to survive the winter drought.

The shape of the conifer needles also prevents another problem that could cause great damage to the trees. Because the needles are round or tapered, snow tends to slide off of them. This generally keeps a heavy buildup of snow from breaking the trees' branches.

The shape of the needles on this blue spruce reduces moisture evaporation, which helps the tree survive the winter drought.

Stepping Lightly or Stamping Through

Animals of the taiga have evolved to develop various adaptations in order to thrive in regions that receive heavy snow. Many taiga animals grow what is the equivalent of snowshoes to enable them to move quickly on the snow. Lynx and snowshoe hares grow extra fur on the bottoms of their paws. This fur not only keeps an animal warmer but also enlarges the size of its paws. The weight of the animal is thus spread out over a larger area, so it is less likely to sink in the soft snow. The extra fur acts like a natural set of snowshoes and helps the animal bound quickly and silently across the newly fallen snow. Widespread toes also contribute to the snowshoe effect.

Larger animals of the taiga move through, rather than over, the snow. Moose have long, stiltlike legs that allow them to keep their bodies above the snow. When walking, moose lift their legs high and place them straight down, in effect punching holes through the snow. In contrast, caribou and bison tend to plow through the snow. One animal takes the lead and breaks a path. The rest of the herd follows, further trampling down the tracks. In this way, the animals make corridors through the snow. Wolves also tend to follow along in each other's paths or along tracks already cleared by caribou or bison.

Large animals, such as this buffalo in Lamar Valley in Yellowstone National Park, plow paths through the deep snow.

DIFFERENT TYPES OF SNOW

The taiga has many different types of snow, and each one has unique characteristics. Each type of snow affects how well different animals survive in the taiga. The Inuit people have names for the different kinds of snow.

The snow that collects on tree branches is called *qali*. The weight of *qali* can cause a young or weak tree to bend toward the ground. If more snow falls, the tree may bend even farther, causing the tender twig tips to nearly touch the ground. Snowshoe hares benefit greatly from this, as it enables them to reach a new source of food. The arches formed by the snow-covered trees also provide the hares with new places in which to hide from many of their predators.

Falling snow is called *annui*. When the fluffly snow has fallen to the ground, it is called *api*. Easy to push aside and move through, this snow is favored by the caribou. They tend to migrate to areas of *api* because they can paw through this soft snow and reach one of their favorite winter foods, the moss that covers the ground.

In the early winter, usually after a few snowfalls, the lower layers of snow take on a loose structure. The ice crystals next to the ground may melt completely. This leaves behind tunnels that small animals can easily crawl through. This loose snow is called *pukak*. Without the *pukak,* mice, voles, shrews, and lemmings could not survive the taiga winter.

Often late in the winter and in the early spring, the top layer of snow melts and then freezes again, forming a thick, icy crust. This hard, slick layer is called *siqoqtoaq*. The *siqoqtoaq* seals the surface of the snow, which prevents air from circulating to the *pukak* tunnels near the ground. To avoid being suffocated, the small mammals that live under the snow must dig tunnels to the surface. There they become easy prey for owls, foxes, and other predators. The *siqoqtoaq* also causes problems for the heavier animals of the taiga, such as moose and caribou. These animals crash through the surface of the snow, gashing their legs on the sharp edges of ice. In many places, their tracks are spotted with blood.

Qali —

Qamaniq

Qali is the Inuit word for snow that rests on tree branches. *Qamaniq* is the Inuit word for the hollow found beneath evergreens that results from snow being intercepted by the tree branches.

A breathing hole, made by a vole, leads down into relatively safe tunnels under the snow. This small mammal spends much of the winter in these compact tunnels.

Life Beneath the Snow

The snow provides a visible record of the activity of many taiga residents. But another world of life lies invisible beneath the snow. Lemmings, shrews, mice, and voles scurry through snow tunnels, sheltered from the predators and the subzero temperatures that would otherwise spell their death.

These tunnels form because the surface of the earth gives off heat, causing a thin layer of snow right above the ground to evaporate. This evaporation creates a narrow tunnel beneath the snow, which acts as a thick layer of insulation. Throughout the winter, the air in these tunnels remains at just below freezing, warm enough to allow the small mammals to thrive in their hidden world. Scurrying through the tunnels, they find plenty of food to last them through the winter. They nibble on plant shoots and seeds on the surface of the ground.

Hidden under the snow, lemmings, shrews, mice, and voles are safe from most of their predators. Some predators, however, can invade this secret world. Minks, martens, and ermine, with their long, sleek bodies, can squeeze through the narrow tunnels and chase the smaller mammals. Foxes sometimes dig into the snow to seize unwary animals. Owls, bears, wolverines, and wolves snatch up the small animals when they poke their heads above the snow.

To make up for the numbers of their populations lost to predators, lemmings, mice, shrews, and voles reproduce rapidly. Lemmings breed many times throughout the winter. A lemming may be a great-great-grandparent by the time the snow melts in the spring.

Small mammals are not the only animals that bear young in the middle of winter. Deep in their dens, female bears give birth to their cubs while blizzards rage in the taiga. The cubs instinctively snuggle against their mothers' fur and begin to nurse. When the days lengthen and the weather warms up, they will emerge from their dens, frisky and strong and ready to greet the spring.

4

Natural Changes in the Taiga

Between 1 million and 2 million years ago, the vast areas of Earth that are now covered by the taiga were leveled by huge sheets of ice called glaciers. The glaciers bowled over trees, dug up the soil, and dragged boulders and rocks for thousands of miles, scouring the land. When the climate warmed up, about 15,000 years ago, the melting glaciers began to retreat. A new land was revealed, a land of cold, sparkling lakes, deeply striated rocks, and long, snaking mounds of gravel. But there was little else. The entire region was devoid of life, having been frozen for more than a million years.

Opposite: The growth of lichen colonies on rock is the first step to forming soil, which eventually will support other plants and animals.

41

The Formation of the Soil

The first step in the evolution of the taiga was the formation of soil on the region's bare rock. As is the case in most other rocky areas, lichens were among the taiga's first inhabitants. Lichens are algae and fungi that live together as a single organism. They were carried by the wind and eventually they settled on rocks, where they formed colorful, sometimes crusty, patches. As they grew, the lichens released chemicals that reacted with the rock, causing tiny flakes of it to break off. The minerals that made up these bits of rock mixed with tiny pieces of dead lichens. The mixture of minerals and organic material formed a tiny amount of soil.

With the formation of small pockets of soil, other organisms became established. Tiny plants called mosses sprouted in soil-filled cracks and depressions in the rock. The mosses continued the process of soil formation started by the lichens. Mosses sent out tiny rootlike structures that grew into the rock's surface. These structures acted like wedges, cracking off tiny bits of rock. More soil accumulated as the minerals from the rock mixed with pieces of the mosses and lichens.

Soon grass seeds, blown in on the wind, began to sprout in the pockets of soil. As the grass grew taller, it caught dust floating through the air. In this way, more and more soil was spread around the plants. The taller grasses also provided shelter for insects, spiders, and other small animals. They provided food for birds and small mammals. The soil became enriched with the organic waste from these animals. In time, a thin layer of soil covered the bare rock. A field—with birds, butterflies, rabbits, and mice, as well as grasses, rushes, and many other plants—carpeted the region where once there was only ice.

From Shrubs to Trees

As the soil grew richer and deeper, shrubs, such as blueberry and willow bushes, sprang up in the sunny field. These plants created shade, which made it difficult for grasses to grow.

FOSSILS OF THE TAIGA

With its permafrost and its peat bogs, the taiga has two powerful ways of preserving organisms. Frozen animal fossils have been found in the permafrost of Siberia and Alaska. The skin and hair of many are intact. The bone marrow remains a healthy white color. The meat of such animals is often so well preserved that it is red with fresh blood. In fact, the meat of one of these frozen animals, a mammoth, was cooked and served to scientists attending a banquet.

Fossil-like remnants have also been preserved in the highly acidic environment of peat bogs. Throughout Europe, the remains of human beings have been found in peat. Like the frozen fossils, these "pickled" fossils are also very well preserved. For example, the brain of one human found in a peat bog in Florida was sealed in the skull, where acids could not get to it. The brain had not decayed at all, and even the genetic material—the DNA—was still intact.

Preserved organic matter can tell us as much about the natural history of an area as this stone fossil, which shows prehistoric plant stems found in Banff National Park, Canada.

Blueberry and spruce show a stunning diversity of autumn color in Alaska's taiga.

Also, the seeds of trees were carried in by birds and other mammals or were blown in on breezes. Trees that thrived in sunny conditions, including pine, aspen, and birch, started growing in the field. The trees shaded the bushes as well as the grasses. Although it may have taken a century or longer in the cold, northern climate, the bright, breezy field eventually became a sun-dappled forest.

The first species of trees to sprout in the new forest did not live for very long, perhaps fifty to one hundred years. Their fallen leaves enriched the soil. Under the canopy of their branches, shade-tolerant trees, including spruce and fir, burgeoned. These trees shot up when the birch, aspen, and pine trees slowly died out. Over many centuries, the taiga gained a foothold across the northern reaches of the Northern Hemisphere.

The taiga became established by a process called succession. During this process, one community of organisms is replaced over time by another and yet another until a stable, long-lasting community—called a climax community—becomes established on the site. The taiga is one of several types of climax communities. The others are the land biomes—the tundra, temperate forest, grassland, tropical rainforest, desert, and chaparral—that along with the taiga cover most of the Earth's continents. Each one is a permanent, self-sustaining community uniquely adapted to the climate and topography of the region in which it is found.

STAGES OF PRIMARY SUCCESSION

Primary succession in bare-rock outcroppings is a very slow process, often requiring hundreds of years.

During the pioneer stages of primary succession, bare rock becomes covered with lichens and mosses. In time, a field grows. Eventually, shrubs and small trees take over the area.

The wind carries seeds of trees, and as succession continues, pine, birch, and aspen trees grow. Where there was once a field, these tall, sun-loving trees quickly dominate.

As shade develops, other types of trees thrive, and a broad-leaf forest eventually comes into being.

Fire and the Taiga

You might think that because the taiga has so many lakes and because the soil of the taiga tends to be soggy that fires would be a rare occurrence there. However, lightning fires are quite common in this biome. In fact, they are a natural force of change in the taiga. Fires occur most often in the summer, when there is less precipitation than there is at other times of the year. The conifer needles that have fallen on the ground dry out. If lightning strikes them, they may ignite in a flash. Flames may then spread across the forest floor, and if they rage long enough and burn hot enough, the trees themselves may ignite.

Fires occur naturally in most parts of the taiga every 50 to 200 years. The fire releases nutrients in the leaf litter of conifer needles. This enriches the soil. The fire also causes the cones of certain

Wildfires can clear land and enrich soil. Soon after a fire, wildflowers and meadow grasses sprout and thrive.

types of pine tree to burst open, releasing the seeds. Very quickly, plants sprout in the burned area. They will follow the pattern of growth that occurred during the later stages of succession, when the taiga was first established. First, a field with grasses, sedges, and wildflowers shoots up. Next, shrubs and tree seedlings begin to dot the landscape. Then, the sun-loving trees, including pine, aspen, and birch, form a young forest. In their shade, the trees of the mature taiga begin to grow and, in time, again become the dominant trees of the forest.

From Lakes to Muskeg to Spruce Forest

About 15,000 years ago, when the glaciers retreated from the region where the taiga now thrives, they left enormous blocks of ice stranded in depressions. As the ice slowly melted, it formed glacial lakes called kettles. Other glacial lakes formed when ice was trapped in a valley blocked with the gravel left behind by a glacier. These lakes usually had no source other than the ice that the glacier had left behind. They were replenished only by runoff from the surrounding area.

At first, these ice-cold lakes were sterile. But dust blowing on the wind landed on the surface of the lakes and sank to the bottom. Over time, a layer of soil formed on the lake bottom. In some of these lakes, the seeds of such water plants as cattails and water lilies landed in the water and sprouted in and around the lake.

In other lakes, however, the spores of a plant called peat moss alighted on the water. These spores did not sink. Instead, they floated on the water's surface. Then, as the spores sprouted, they formed a mat of peat moss near the edge of the lake. Peat moss contains gas-filled cells that allow the plants to float.

As the peat moss grew upward, older parts of the plants were pushed under the water. The gas bubbled out of the peat moss, and the cells filled with water. The dead, soggy moss sank to the bottom of the lake, where it rotted slowly in the cold water. As it rotted, it released acids that turned the water brown. These acids made it difficult for any other plants to grow in the lake.

The peat moss, however, thrived. It formed a thick, moist mat around the edge of the lake. Over time, the peat moss spread toward the center and covered the entire lake. This blanket of moss prevented the sun from warming the cold, brown, acidic water below.

While the peat moss spread slowly across the lake, another process was occurring that quickened the gradual

47

FROM PEAT TO COAL

In a few hundred million years, today's peat bogs in the taiga, and in other regions, may be mined for their fossil fuels. Peat is the first step in the formation of coal. In places where coal is rare, peat is sometimes burned for fuel. This light brown, spongy material is dug up from swamps, dried, and cut into blocks. When they are burned, the peat blocks give off a lot of smoke.

A cleaner-burning fuel called lignite forms if peat bogs are covered with thick sediments and left undisturbed for a few million years. The weight of the sediments compresses the peat, and the moisture in it is pressed out. The peat hardens over time and changes into lignite, the softest form of coal. Compared to peat, lignite emits very little smoke when it burns.

If the lignite remains buried for a hundred million years or more, and if additional layers of sand, rock, and water press down on it, it changes into bituminous coal. This soft, black coal is the most common fossil fuel in the United States. It burns hotter and cleaner than lignite and is often used to create the steam that powers turbines in electric power plants.

Given enough time and pressure, bituminous coal becomes anthracite. This extremely hard coal gives off very little smoke when it is burned. However, anthracite is the rarest form of coal. Deposits of anthracite are often buried very deep in the ground and are, thus, difficult to mine. The entire process from peat bog to anthracite deposit may take 400 million years or more.

Peat may need more than a hundred million years to change first to lignite and then to bituminous coal. The black seam shown is lignite.

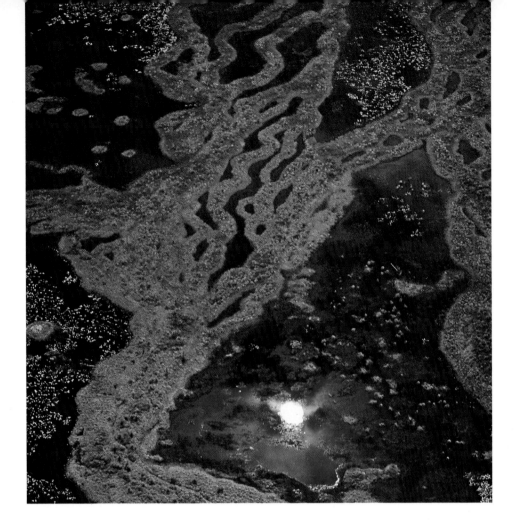

An aerial view catches the sun's sparkling reflection in the water of the muskeg on Hamilton Inlet in Labrador, Canada.

process of succession. Even when the mat of peat moss was very thin, dust and soil landed on its surface. Other plants shot up in the pockets of moss-moistened soil. The peat moss sprouted a floating garden that included grasses and flowers, laurel bushes, willow thickets, and small spruce trees. This region, with its trees tilting crazily in the not-quite-firm ground, is known as the muskeg.

The muskeg is a common feature of the taiga landscape. But in some parts of the taiga, the lakes underneath the muskeg have filled in entirely with decaying peat. The spruce trees, which up to this point have grown slowly because nutrients available from the peat moss on which they grew have been limited, can now shoot up more rapidly. They can send roots into the solid peat. They can grow closer together, and they will not sink. The muskeg gradually becomes a mature spruce forest.

5

Threats to the Taiga

The destruction of the rainforest has been a well-publicized problem for many years. Few people realize, however, that the boreal forest—the taiga—is equally threatened. Large tracts of land across north-central Canada and Russia have been leased to giant lumber and paper companies. Many of these companies harvest wood by clear-cutting—chopping down all the trees in an area. Scientists and others worry that in the harsh northern climate, the taiga will not ever be able to grow back. Overdevelopment of the taiga's resources of wild game, lumber, and minerals is not just a problem of this century. It has been a problem for several hundred years.

51

Threats to the Animals

In the centuries before Europeans settled on the North American continent, millions of beavers waddled across the taiga. Their dam building and tree felling helped give shape to the forest. By building dams, they tamed rapids, flooded marshes, and maintained clearings that gave birch and aspen trees an advantage over spruce trees in scattered areas across the northern woods.

Beaver fur was highly valued by European hat makers because it is thick, waterproof, and makes a firm, pliable felt that can easily be shaped into high-fashion hats. Native Americans began trading beaver furs for manufactured goods, and by the early 1600s, a rich trade had become established across northern North America. Over the next 150 years, beavers in the north woods were hunted so extensively by Native Americans and Europeans that they almost became extinct. There are limits on trapping beavers today, and their numbers have increased in most areas of the taiga. However, the beaver population will probably never again be what it was in the days before the European settlement of North America.

In the mid- and late 1800s, hunters also almost wiped out the huge herds of wood bison that once grazed in the grassy marshes that dot the taiga. In 1922, the Canadian government set aside a large expanse of northern land as Wood Buffalo National Park. There were probably fewer than a thousand of these dark, shaggy creatures left in the region. Over the past seventy years, however, the bison populations have recovered. Now more than 15,000 wood bison roam the park.

Wood Buffalo National Park has served as a refuge for other animals besides wood bison. Peregrine falcons and bald eagles have thrived here; in other parts of the continent, they have been endangered. The park also contains the only nesting ground of America's rarest bird, the whooping crane. In Russia, the taiga serves as resting and nesting grounds for the equally endangered Siberian cranes. Still, these magnificent,

Whooping cranes are among the animals of the taiga that are endangered.

THE ENDANGERED AMUR TIGER

The world's largest feline, the Amur or Siberian tiger, is an inhabitant of the taiga in far eastern Russia. These stunning animals are gravely in danger of extinction in the wild. But they continue to be hunted relentlessly across their range.

Although the Amur tiger is endangered, its meat is highly prized in China, Korea, and Japan, not so much for its flavor but for use in "love potions." Its pelt is made into luxurious, although illegal, rugs. The tiger—skin, body parts, and all—may sell for $8,000. The average Russian has an annual income of $800 or less. Because the demand is so great, the poachers (illegal hunters) are so poor, and the remote border between Russia and China and North Korea is rarely patrolled, the tigers have little chance of surviving if steps to protect them are not taken soon.

Scientists and conservationists from around the world have been working together to try to save the Amur tiger. They monitor the tiger population by putting radio collars on the animals and then tracking them. They patrol the nature preserves in an attempt to discourage poaching. They work to convince the local people that the tigers are a tourist attraction and, therefore, worth more alive than dead. Nonetheless, fifty tigers were killed in 1992 alone. At this rate, the Amur tigers will be wiped out within five to ten years. The survivors—about 250 to 400—will be all that remain of this beautiful animal, symbolic of fierce power, stealth, and pride.

An Amur, or Siberian, tiger cub nuzzles its mother. There are only between 250 and 400 of these animals left in the world.

large birds are threatened by hunters, who sometimes shoot them down by accident. These birds are also threatened by pollution or destruction of the marshes of the taiga, the only place where they breed in the wild.

Threats to the Trees

In the 1600s, the forests on the southern edges of the taiga were dominated by stands of white pines more than 100 feet (30 meters) tall and more than 300 years old. These giants grew straight and tall—and made perfects masts for the sailing ships of the 1700s and 1800s. The colonists who settled in eastern Canada harvested the white pines so thoroughly that few are left in the region. There are isolated white-pine forests in Canada's provincial parks and near the northern shores of Lake Superior. However, even these forests are threatened by logging and diseases. The stately forests of white pine trees reaching up to the sky may be wiped out in our lifetime.

Today, logging imperils the spruce forests all across the taiga region. Spruce trees do not grow as tall as the towering white pines of the southern taiga. But the fibers that make up the wood are very strong, so spruce logs can be shaved and treated to produce high-quality wood pulp for making paper. The demand for paper and paper products is constantly growing. Unless we begin buying more products made of recycled paper, the taiga's spruce trees may be chopped down and ground up before we know it. The loss of this biome will be the price we pay for our frequent use of products such as paper plates, paper towels, tissues, and disposable diapers.

We have more than our intentional destruction of the taiga to worry about. We are destroying the taiga unintentionally as well, by means of a silent killer called acid rain. Acid rain forms when certain pollutants—such as sulfur dioxide, which is released when coal is burned, and nitrogen oxide, which is released when gasoline is burned—mix with water vapor in the clouds. The precipitation that falls from these clouds is acidic.

Acid rain has destroyed vast stretches of taiga in some parts of Europe.

When acid rain falls on the spruce and pine trees of the taiga, it can damage the needles of these trees. It also seeps into the soil, where it damages the trees' roots. In some parts of northern Russia and Scandinavia, entire areas of the taiga have slowly died off because of acid rain. The dead trees stand like gray skeletons against the sky.

MAKING TREES INTO PAPER

If you tear off a corner of a piece of paper and look at the torn corner with a magnifying glass, you will see tiny fibers poking out in all directions. These fibers come from trees, often trees of the taiga.

The first step in making paper occurs when loggers travel to areas of the taiga that have been slated for cutting. Using a chain saw for chopping down individual trees, or bulldozers for clear-cutting, the trees are felled. If good logging roads have been built, the trees may be loaded on large trucks and carried to mills. If a fairly large stream or river runs nearby, the logs may be tagged and floated down the waterway. When they reach the vicinity of a pulping mill, they will be hauled in, sorted, and stripped for their bark. The wood will then be shaved into chips, which may be soaked in water and ground into tiny pieces to make pulp. The chips may also be soaked in chemicals and cooked over high heat. In either case, the result is wood pulp.

The wood pulp is usually bleached to make it white. Then it is poured onto a fine screen that collects the fibers while allowing the water to drip through. Rollers press the fibers together, forcing even more water out of the emerging paper. Finally, the paper dries and is wound onto large rolls. Paper sheets of various sizes are cut from these rolls.

An enormous mound of wood chips, shown here at a paper mill in Texas. Using recycled paper will lessen the need to cut new trees for paper.

Threats to the Land and Water

Destruction of the taiga does not threaten only the trees and the wildlife of the region. It threatens the health of the entire ecosystem. For instance, when large stands of trees are logged in a clear-cut, no plants remain to anchor the soil. A heavy rain may wash away the soil in the area. The taiga cannot easily grow back in the eroded area, which may remain bare for many, many years.

The soil that washes away from what used to be the taiga chokes the clear-running streams and rivers. Fish that require cold, fast-moving water, such as salmon, can no longer thrive there. The biome becomes further impoverished.

Water pollution from erosion, however, is minor when compared to the pollution caused by wood-pulping mills and mines in the taiga. These industries dump their wastes into nearby rivers, turning the water dark brown. Animals downstream from the pulp mills often avoid drinking the water, and people who fish for sport may decide not to eat what they catch. Mining releases dangerous pollutants called heavy metals into the soil. Animals that feed on plants growing in the polluted soil may become poisoned and die. In some parts of Russia near nickel smelters, 400 years may pass before the soil is free of these deadly pollutants.

Threats to the Earth

Destruction of the taiga could cause problems in all of the Earth's biomes by disrupting the climate worldwide. Such disruption would be related to changes in the Earth's atmosphere. Gases in the Earth's atmosphere, including carbon dioxide, help trap the sun's heat close to the planet. This process is known as the greenhouse effect. The greenhouse effect enables the Earth to stay warm enough for many different life forms to thrive.

In recent years, however, there has been a buildup of greenhouse gasses in our atmosphere. This buildup is due in part to the burning of fossil fuels, which releases carbon dioxide and other gases into the air. A thicker layer of these gases may trap extra heat near the Earth, causing global warming.

The taiga, like other forests, helps reduce the amount of carbon dioxide in the atmosphere. During photosynthesis, the trees that inhabit this biome take in carbon dioxide to make sugar. When the taiga is destroyed, there are fewer trees to absorb the carbon dioxide, and the levels of this gas go up. As a result, our planet may warm up relatively quickly, causing many different types of plants and animals to become extinct.

For many people, the taiga is a biome that is out of sight and, therefore, out of mind. But we use the taiga's resources every day. It provides us with wood, paper, and essential minerals. Many people depend on the taiga to supply clean water. The taiga provides shelter for a diverse set of animals. It helps keep our global climate under control. The taiga is a great green belt ringing the top of the world—a biome that we can ill afford to despoil or destroy.

Glossary

acid rain Precipitation with a high acid content that results when rain mixes with gases that are released when petroleum products are burned.

adaptation A characteristic of an organism that makes it suited to live or reproduce in a particular environment.

atmosphere The layer of gases that surrounds the Earth.

biome A community of specific types of plants, animals, and other organisms that covers a large area of the Earth.

camouflage To blend in with the surroundings, especially by matching the color or shapes of the background.

coniferous trees Trees that bear cones. Most conifers are evergreen and bear needle-shaped leaves.

deciduous trees Trees that drop their leaves in the fall.

decomposition The process by which bacteria and other organisms break down dead plants and animals to release the organic materials they contain.

dormancy A state of inactivity in a plant, during which no growth occurs and metabolic processes are minimal.

estivation A state of deep sleep in the summer, during which an animal's body temperature and breathing rate drops to help prevent it from overheating or becoming dehydrated.

evergreen Having leaves or needles throughout the year.

extinction The dying out of a species.

food web A diagram that shows the feeding relationships among all the different organisms in a community.

glacier A thick sheet of ice that covers an area of land. Glaciers once covered much of the region that is now the taiga.

hibernation A state of deep sleep in which body temperature and heart rate drop very low. Some taiga animals hibernate during the winter to help them survive the cold.

insulate To hold a steady temperature.

krummholz A forest of willow, birch, and evergreen trees, all less than a few feet tall, that separates the taiga from the tundra region.

larva The immature form of an insect that has not yet metamorphosed, or changed to its adult form.

lichen An association of algae and fungi living together as a single unit.

migrate To move seasonally or periodically, from one region or climate to another.

muskeg An acidic bog of the taiga, which may be covered with bushes or even small trees.

organic material Any substance that comes from a living organism and that contains carbon.

organism Any living thing, such as a plant, an animal, a fungus, or a bacterium.

permafrost A layer of permanently frozen ground that lies beneath the tundra surface. It also exists in patches in the taiga.

photosynthesis The process by which plants use the energy from sunlight to make sugars, which they use for food.

pollutants Harmful chemicals that are released into the air, the water, or onto the land.

predator An animal that hunts other animals to eat them.

prey An animal that is eaten by another animal.

pupa An insect in the intermediate stage of development, after the larva and before the adult.

reproduction The process by which an organism creates new individuals of the same species.

species A group of animals or plants whose members can interbreed and produce fertile offspring.

succession A natural process that occurs over time by which one community of organisms is replaced by other communities until a stable, long-lasting community, called a climax community, is established.

For Further Reading

Asimov, Isaac. *What Causes Acid Rain?* Milwaukee: Gareth Stevens, 1992.

_____. *Is Our Planet Warming Up?* Milwaukee: Gareth Stevens, 1992.

Asimov, Isaac, and Kaplan, Elizabeth. *How Is Paper Made?* Milwaukee: Gareth Stevens, 1993.

Greenaway, Theresa. *Fir Trees.* Chatham, NJ: Raintree Steck-Vaughn Publishers, 1990.

Hora, Bayard, ed. *Trees and Forests of the World* (2 volumes). New York: Marshall Cavendish, 1990.

Kaplan, Elizabeth. *Tundra.* New York: Marshall Cavendish, 1996.

Leggett, Jeremy. *Dying Forests.* New York: Marshall Cavendish, 1991.

Milne, Lorus J., and Milner, Margery. *The Mystery of the Bog Forest.* New York: Dodd, Mead & Company, 1989.

Paige, David. *A Day in the Life of a Forest Ranger.* Mahwah, NJ: Troll Associates, 1980.

Radlauer, Ruth, and Gitkin, Lisa S. *The Power of Ice.* Chicago: Childrens Press, 1985.

Schoonmaker, Peter K. *The Living Forest.* Hillside, NJ: Enslow Publishers, Inc., 1990.

Stille, Darlene R. *Ice Age.* Chicago: Childrens Press, 1990.

Williams, Terry Tempest, and Major, Ted. *The Secret Language of Snow.* New York: Pantheon Books, 1984.

Index

Acknowledgments and Photo Credits
Cover: ©Michael Giannechini/Photo Researchers, Inc.; page 6: ©Paolo Koch/Photo Researchers, Inc.;
p. 9: ©Rod Planck/Photo Researchers, Inc.; p. 10: ©F. Stuart Westmorland/Photo Researchers, Inc.; p.
12: ©John Lemker/Earth Scenes; p. 14: ©Gregory K. Scott/Photo Researchers, Inc.; p. 15: ©Zig
Leszczynski/Earth Scenes; p. 16: ©Ed Reschke/Peter Arnold, Inc.; pp. 18, 25, 30: ©Johnny Johnson/
Animals Animals; p. 20: ©Ed Cesar/Photo Researchers, Inc.; p. 21: ©William Bacon III/Photo
Researchers, Inc.; p. 22: ©Mark Newman/Photo Researchers, Inc.; pp. 24, 31: ©Tom & Pat Leeson/
Photo Researchers, Inc.; p. 28: ©John Kieffer/Peter Arnold, Inc.; p. 33: ©E. R. Degginger/Photo
Researchers, Inc.; p. 35: ©Breck P. Kent/Earth Scenes; p. 36: ©Jim Zipp/Photo Researchers, Inc.; p.
38: ©Virginia Weinland/Photo Researchers, Inc.; p. 40: ©S. J. Krasemann/Peter Arnold, Inc.; p. 43:
©Patti Murray/Earth Scenes; p. 44: ©Michael Giannechini/Photo Researchers, Inc.; p. 46:
©Degginger/Earth Scenes; p. 48: ©David J. Cross/Peter Arnold, Inc.; p. 49: ©John Eastcott/YVA
Momatiuk/Earth Scenes; p. 50: ©Francis Lepine/Earth Scenes; p. 53: ©Ray Richardson/Animals
Animals; p. 54: ©Zig Leszczynski/Animals Animals; p. 56: ©Richard Packwood/Earth Scenes; p. 57:
©Tom Hollyman/Photo Researchers, Inc.
Artwork by Blackbirch Graphics, Inc.